Disease and Discovery

Eva Bailey

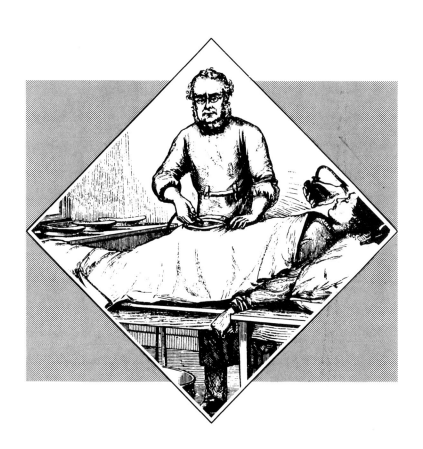

Batsford Academic and Educational   London

Typeset by Tek-Art Ltd, Kent
and printed in Great Britain
by R.J. Acford
Chichester, Sussex
for the publishers
Batsford Academic and Educational,
an imprint of B. T. Batsford Ltd,
4 Fitzhardinge Street
London W1H 0AH

ISBN 0 7134 4633 1

ACKNOWLEDGMENT

The author would like to thank Professor
C.S.F. Easmon of the Wright Fleming
Institute and G.F. Harris of the British
Leprosy Relief Association for helpful
suggestions.

The Author and Publishers would like to
thank the following for their kind permission
to reproduce copyright illustrations: Austra-
lian Atomic Energy Commission, fig. 52;
British Library, fig. 9; British School of Os-
teopathy, fig. 60; Central Office of Information
(Crown copyright reserved), fig. 58; Design
Team Partnership, fig. 46; Health Education
Council, fig. 59; Keystone Press Agency, figs
14, 21, 50; Liverpool Corporation, fig. 32; Pat-
ricia Mandel, fig. 25; The Mansell
Collection, figs 2, 8, 11, 12, 15, 19, 26, 28, 30,
34, 38, 40, 41, 42, 43, 44, 45, 47; Marshall
Cavendish, fig. 1; Mary Evans Picture
Library, figs. 5, 10, 22, 33; Medical Illustration
Dept, John Radcliffe Hospital, Headington,
Oxford, figs 23, 24, 29, 37, 57; National
Portrait Gallery, fig. 16; Press Association,
figs 54, 56; St Mary's Hospital Medical School,
fig. 48; Graham and Jacquie Sergeant, fig. 49;
Times Newspapers Ltd, figs 6, 7, 51, 55;
Wellcome Institute Library, figs 20, 36, 39;
University College Hospital, fig. 35; World
Health Organization, fig. 53. Figures 18, 27,
31 and 61 are from the Publishers' collection.
Diagrams 3 and 17 were drawn by R.F. Brien.
The picture research was by Patricia Mandel.

Contents

The Illustrations

1
Early Times

"Take one 5 ml. spoonful three times a day."

How often have you been instructed to take a dose of medicine in this way? It was not always so.

The medicines and the treatments we are given today are the result of centuries of study, observation and care by dedicated medical and scientific experts.

Curses and Spells

Early man, in his attempt to understand unaccountable illnesses, turned to superstition, magic and religion to explain his suffering and seek a cure. If someone was stricken with a weakening fever, his friends would be quick to tell him, "You must have angered the gods." Death was often regarded as the penalty for sin. It was said that those suffering mental illness were possessed by an evil spirit. Infection, poisoning and the breakdown of bodily functions were not recognized as illnesses.

Sometimes a person born with a physical deformity was considered to be endowed with magic by which others could be cured. Another superstition insisted that the seventh son of a seventh son had powers of healing.

Outside influences such as the sun, the moon, precious metals and gems were believed to hold control over disease by healing or warding off a dreaded sickness.

Medicines and cures were often concocted from plants, insects and parts of animals. Sometimes they worked and sometimes they did not.

Hippocrates

On the Greek island of Cos in about the year 400 BC, Hippocrates was studying healing and medicine in a very different way. He refused to accept that illness was controlled by remote powers. By following a scientific approach, Hippocrates sought to prove that natural causes were responsible for all illnesses. He considered the progress of each illness he came across and carefully recorded what he found.

Hippocrates taught his methods of studying medicine to others. Very high standards and ideals were insisted upon. The importance of being careful and accurate in carrying out and recording their work was stressed to the students.

Even in his lifetime Hippocrates was known as Hippocrates the Great, and in the centuries since his death he has been called The Father of Medicine.

The Hippocratic Method rejected the old superstitious beliefs. It concentrated on understanding disease. Hippocrates studied the prognosis (what is likely to happen) as an illness takes its course. Hippocrates regarded people with mental disorders as sick people, and did not consider them to be possessed by evil spirits. It was not until the seventeenth century that what he taught began to be accepted.

1 Different versions of the Hippocratic Oath have been used over the centuries, but all demand the same high standard of service and purity of living. This copy of a medieval translation of the Oath shows the snake of Aesculapius entwined round the illuminated first letter.

The findings regarding all the illnesses studied were very carefully recorded. They are still read and referred to today by the medical profession. In the nineteenth century, an enormous advance in medical knowledge took place, the basis of which was the work recorded by Hippocrates, together with those writings which, although they may not actually have been his work, were attributed to him.

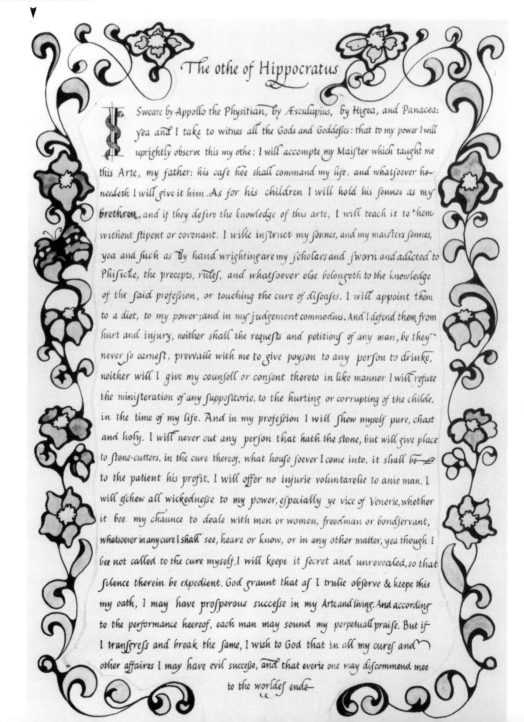

The othe of Hippocratus

I Sweare by Appollo the Physitian, by Aesculapius, by Higea, and Panacea: yea and I take to witnes all the Gods and Goddesses: that to my power I will uprightly observe this my othe: I will accompte my Maister which taught me this Arte, my father: his case hee shall command my life. and whatsoever he needeth I will give it him. As for his children I will hold his sonnes as my brethren, and if they desire the knowledge of this arte, I will teach it to them without stipent or covenant. I wille instruct my sonnes, and my maisters sonnes, yea and such as by hand wrighting are my scholars and sworn and adicted to Phisicke, the precepts, rules, and whatsoever else belongeth to the knowledge of the said profession, or touching the cure of diseases. I will appoint them to a diet, to my power; and in my judgement commodius. And I defend them from hurt and injury, neither shall the requests and petitions of any man, be they never so earnest, prevvaile with me to give poyson to any person to drinke, neither will I give my counsell or consent thereto in like manner I will refute the ministeration of any suppositorie. to the hurting or corrupting of the childe, in the time of my life. And in my profession I will shew myself pure, chast and holy. I will never cut any person that hath the stone, but will give place to stone-cutters, in the cure thereof, what house soever I come into, it shall be to the patient his profit. I will offer no injurie voluntarelie to anie man. I will eschew all wickednesse to my power, especially ye vice of Venerie, whether it bee my chaunce to deale with men or women, freedman or bondservant, whatsoever in any cure I shall see, heare or know, or in any other matter, yea though I bee not called to the cure myself, I will keepe it secret and unrevealed, so that silence therein be expedient. God graunt that as I trulie observe & keepe this my oath, I may have prosperous successe in my Arte and living. And according to the performance heereof, each man may sound my perpetuall praise. But if I transgress and break the same, I wish to God that in all my cures and other affaires I may have evil successe, and that everie one may discommend mee to the worldes ende

The Hippocratic Oath

All who undertook medical work as pupils of Hippocrates were required to swear an oath, pledging themselves to high standards of morals and a dedication to their work. This is known as the Hippocratic Oath. It lays down the requirement for doctors to help and befriend others in the profession. The following instructions regarding a doctor's life and his relationship with his patients are included:

I swear and I vow . . .

I will follow that method of treatment which, according to my ability and judgment, I consider for the benefit of my patients, and abstain from whatever is deleterious and mischievous . . . .

With purity and with holiness I will pass my life and practise my art . . . . Into whatever houses I enter I will go into them for the benefit of the sick and will abstain from every voluntary act of mischief and corruption . . . .

Whatever, in connection with my professional practice, or not in connection with it, I may see or hear in the lives of men which ought not to be spoken abroad, I will not divulge, counting such things to be as sacred secrets.

While I continue to keep this oath unviolated may it be granted to me to enjoy life and the practice of the art, respected by all men at all times, but should I trespass and violate this oath, may the reverse be my lot.

This famous Oath still sets the standard of medical conduct throughout the world, and is accepted and adhered to in Britain. When a newly qualified British doctor presents himself or herself at the inaugural ceremony before practising medicine, the Hippocratic Oath is usually included in the proceedings. Any doctor who breaks the Oath is struck off the medical register of doctors and not allowed to practise medicine.

2 This statue shows Aesculapius, the Greek god of healing, holding his staff around which is entwined a snake.

The Snake of Aesculapius

The Greek god of healing was Aesculapius. In the area around the Temple of Healing at Cos, erected in honour of Aesculapius, Hippocrates and his associates studied and practised medicine. The methods of Hippocrates were

A

3 This badge was commonly displayed on doctors' cars some years ago.

4 Today, a simple, stylized staff and snake form the symbol of the British Medical Association.

▼

5 Nuns help to care for and comfort the sick in this medieval hospital.

very different from the ritualistic ceremonie which took place in the Temple of Healing.

The symbol of the god Aesculapius was snake twined round a staff. This is still th emblem of the medical profession in Britai today. The snake is able to cast off a dead skir revealing a newly grown one beneath. Thi symbolizes renewal.

The Work of the Monks

Just as the Greeks practised medicine i temples dedicated to their god of healing, so, i Christian times, it was under the influence c religion that the care of the sick took place. Fo 500 years after William of Normand conquered England in 1066, monks formed th medical profession of the country. Unlik Hippocrates and his followers, the monks wer not trained scientifically, nor did the investigate illness in the same way. Thei work was much more practical. The sick wer comforted and cared for, their pain was ease and injuries gently tended.

The monks originally made provision onl for sick members of their community. The then began to add small buildings to thei monastic settlements in order that they coul care for ordinary men and women. The mon called the Infirmarian was in charge of thos who were sick. The room in the monaster infirmary where patients were cared for wa an early version of many hospital wards w know today.

Especially in the infirmaries and in th public hospitals which were built later, nun looked after the patients. They were the sister of a religious order. Today, the highly skille nurse in charge of a hospital ward is still calle "Sister".

6 Today, a highly qualified Sister is in charge of a ward at St Thomas's Hospital, London. The original hospital was founded in 1215.

Early Hospitals

Two London hospitals which are famous today were founded in the Middle Ages. The building of St Bartholomew's began in 1123 and St Thomas's in 1215. At first these hospitals offered shelter, food and loving care, but little medical attention.

7 Outside St Bartholomew's Hospital, London. The original structure was begun in 1123.
▼

2
Plague
and Pestilence

The study and practice of medicine progressed little during the Middle Ages. Monks travelling to Britain from the Continent brought with them herbs known to have healing properties. These were cultivated in special herb gardens and from the plants some of the first medicines were made.

Those who travelled also brought recipes for cures. Remedies already known and the new ones were collected together. During the tenth century, Bald's *Leechbook* was compiled. A leech is a type of small worm which has suckers at both ends. It feeds on the blood of animals. It was used in medicine for many centuries to "draw" the blood of humans for various reasons. Bald's collection of remedies included several herbal recipes sent by the Patriarch of Jerusalem.

8 Herb gardens like this were carefully tended in earlier centuries, so that an adequate supply of medicinal plants was always available to make herbal medicines.
▼

The Spread of Disease

Travellers to Britain were also the carriers of illness from other countries. In the eleventh century, returning crusaders introduced diseases previously unknown in Britain. Two of these were leprosy and smallpox. In the Middle Ages there was a major epidemic of leprosy and a few centuries later smallpox was to become the scourge of man.

Although the leprosy suffered was not always the severe form known today, once people had contracted signs of the scaly skin disease they were regarded as outcasts. The disease spread so easily that the sufferers were completely shunned by all other people.

The treatment of the sufferers was callous and cruel. They were regarded as no longer living. Mass for the dead was said for them in the churches. The lepers were required to wear dark clothing and to warn everyone of their coming by the sound of a bell or a clapper.

Even the monks refused to admit lepers inside their premises, but they were not entirely uncaring. At some monasteries, grain was stored in barns belonging to the religious order. At one end of the barn, the monks added a small chamber in the form of a tiny room. A small stone chute was built into the wall. From the inside of the almshouse, the monks poured corn down the chute to the lepers waiting outside. If the monks were unable to treat the disease of leprosy, they did endeavour to prevent the victims from dying of hunger.

Since the lepers were shunned to such a degree, they tended to group together, living apart from the leprosy-free population.

The total exclusion of any sufferer from leprosy was a very severe measure. While it was outrageous as far as caring for the sick was concerned, it was because of these restrictions that the disease of leprosy was largely stamped out in England and other parts of Europe.

Today, although many cases of leprosy throughout the world have been cured by treatment with a drug, there is now the problem of drug resistance. The drug dapsone has been overcoming leprosy since it was first used in the 1940s. Unfortunately it is no longer effective on its own. Treatment for leprosy is a slow process, carried out over many years. Careful checks are constantly made to ensure that the drugs are still effective. There are very few cases of leprosy in Britain today. This problem is now being investigated by the World Health Organisation and a combination of drugs is being recommended.

9   A leper, wearing dark clothes and ringing his warning bell. Look at all the spots on his face.

Lack of Hygiene

Filth and unhygienic conditions were frequent causes of illness during the Middle Ages. It was an accepted habit to discard household rubbish of any kind by throwing it through the window and into the street. Since the houses were built very close together, there was an immediate health hazard. Sanitary provision was non-existent, and rotting vegetation gave ff bad smells. Even pure water flowing from springs and streams was polluted by rubbish being thrown into it. Germs multiplied and caused outbreaks of plague, leprosy, smallpox and other illnesses.

The Black Death

One of the diseases most feared was bubonic plague. It caused much suffering and the death rate was high. Plague was caused by the bite of a flea which was carried in the fur of the black rat. The disease was easily passed on to man, and dirt and filth contributed to its rapid spread. It was not until 1894 that the cause of the disease was discovered.

Between 1348 and 1350, plague swept the country to such an extent that it was called the Black Death. It is thought it was so-called because people who caught bubonic plague developed black glandular swellings in the armpits and groin, in addition to suffering the usual symptoms of fever.

About half the population of London died, and it was estimated that about one third of the people in the whole of the country were wiped out by plague. The few people who survived, and who had previously only grown crops on strips of land in the open fields, were able to take over the land of others who had died and add it to their own. In this way they became tenant farmers.

No longer were the monks the only cultivators of herb gardens. Since the new farmers worked more land, they were able to set aside plots near to their cottages on which to grow herbs. Gradually the housewife increased her knowledge of the soothing and healing properties of herbs, in addition to using the plants in cooking. Her knowledge had to be accurate, for some herbs, such as Hemlock and Fools' Parsley, are poisonous to man.

The Dissolution of the Monasteries

The whole system of monastic medical care collapsed when Henry VIII ordered the dissolution of the monasteries. This took place during the period 1536-39. Buildings were wrecked, including monastic infirmaries, the monks fled and the herb gardens were abandoned.

The situation became impossible. The housewife had only limited knowledge. Those who were ill, injured, or dying of poverty or old age could no longer turn to the monks for nursing care. Travellers who took ill on their journey were stranded. Even wounded soldiers returning from fighting were unable to have their injuries attended to.

Both St Bartholomew's and St Thomas's Hospitals were closed. King Henry relented somewhat and allowed St Bartholomew's Hospital, but not the monastery to which it was attached, to re-open. St Thomas's Hospital was to remain closed until shortly before the death of Edward VI in 1553.

The hospital system in Britain was practically non-existent. Housewives were able to cope with everyday illnesses, but not with anything more serious.

Herbs

As time went on, more 'herbals' – collections of recipes using herbs – began and continued to appear. Those who could read gained some knowledge from these. In the sixteenth century various collections which were compiled included *The Little Herbal* by Anthony Askham, *The New Herbal* by Turner, Henry Lyte's *Herbal*, and a book which became very famous, *The Herbal* by John Gerard. These books included recipes for using herbs for cooking, medicinal and other purposes. William Coles wrote *The Art of Simpling*. A simple is a medicinal herb.

But how did people obtain remedies for their ills? Some turned to the "wise women" who had, by now, an extensive knowledge of the soothing and healing properties of herbs.

Quacks

Boastful men loudly proclaimed their own

11   Quacks were not only found in Britain. This famous
picture, showing the impostor trying to persuade
innocent people that he could cure their ills, is by the
Dutch painter, Jan Steen (1626-79).

pposed abilities and professed to be doctors.
hey enticed people to pay them for
nsultations and cures.

It was a sham. These men had not received
ny training in medical skills. They stood in
arket places and at street corners. While
ey claimed to have studied medicine and to
 able to cure all kinds of ailments, they were
ten illiterate. Since their wordy cry was
kened to the quack of a duck, they became
nown as "quacks". The pills, liniments, salves
d medicines they sold were highly priced.
eople bought their wares, some believing the
postor's patter, others anxious to try
ything to relieve their pain. The quacks
grew rich and moved on, but they did little to
cure the sick.

The Divine Right of Kings

It was believed for many centuries that the
kings and queens of England reigned by
Divine Right and that God had put each, in
turn, on the throne. Because of this, not only
was it thought that the king or queen could do
no wrong, but the monarch was also
considered to be endowed with the power to
cure illness. Sick people were brought before
the monarch at a special audience. It was

15

hoped that the God-given gift in the royal touch would restore good health. Scrofula (tuberculosis of the neck glands) was called "The King's Evil". It was believed that the monarch could cure this disease. Until the end of the reign of Queen Anne in 1714, people were granted permits to attend the royal residence so that they could be touched by the monarch in the hope that they would be healed.

The Doctrine of Signatures

A great advance in herbal medicine was thought to have appeared when the Doctrine of Signatures became known. An Italian inventor named Della Porta published a book called *Phytognomonica* in 1588. In it he described how illnesses like jaundice, which give the skin a yellow cast, would be cured by a yellow flower, heart disease would be cured by plants with heart-shaped leaves, and plants with red blossoms or red marks on their stems or leaves would purify the blood. The idea was to connect the sign (signature) between the illness and the plant or herb which would cure it.

This method was widely practised by herbalists and other medical practitioners for about a century. Since there was no scientific explanation for cures, any success must have been coincidental, possibly being brought about by the faith of the patient.

Nicholas Culpeper (1616-54)

In 1652, Nicholas Culpeper published a book called *The English Physician* and in 1653 another called *The Complete Herbal*. Culpeper was a Roundhead, a herbalist and also an astrologer. He believed that the planets influenced all nature and therefore all herbs. Culpeper gave instructions for certain herbs to be picked at sunrise, or when the moon was new, or when certain signs of the zodiac were considered to be in the ascendancy. The instructions given in Culpeper's books could also be attributed to the use of common sense. The time of gathering would depend on whether young leaves or ripe fruits of a plant were required, and these would be available at different times of the gardening year.

The Great Plague

All the efforts to overcome sickness and disease failed to stem yet another onslaught of bubonic plague, or the Pestilence, as it was then frequently called. After a series of small outbreaks, in 1665 an epidemic swept London and other parts of the country. It was of such great proportions that it was called the Great Plague.

Although, at the time, the cause of bubonic plague was not known, people were well aware

◀ **12** Nicholas Culpeper (1616-54). He supported the Roundheads, and was a herbalist who applied astrology to the preparation of his remedies.

13 Rich people had perfumed balls, similar to this, fashioned in precious metals such as gold or silver. The word "pomander" comes from the French word "pomme", meaning "apple".

smelling flowers, herbs and spices they contained released their perfume. The dried flowers and herbs which the pomander held included scented rose petals, lavender and bay leaves. Cinnamon was one of the spices. The mixture was called "pot-pourri". The poor person's version of a pomander was an orange stuck with cloves.

It was believed that by inhaling pleasant smells and keeping the surrounding air fragrant, disease, as well as unpleasant smells, would be kept away.

Varous kinds of pomanders and pot-pourri are still made and sold today, but they are now used to impart their pleasant scent and not as a possible preventive against disease. We still use air fresheners in our homes.

In the seventeenth century, men and women also carried sprigs of herbs or posies of sweet-scented flowers to help, as they thought, to keep disease away. Since they were intended to be smelled, these were termed "nosegays". This is the origin of the tradition that the Queen and other members of the royal family are presented with flowers as they carry out official engagements.

Herbs, spices and flowers did nothing to control the plague. People realized they had caught the disease when they became feverish and had fits of sneezing. Glandular swellings quickly appeared and soon the victim was dead. This is recorded in the well-known children's singing game, which describes the disease:

Ring a ring of roses,
A pocketful of posies,
A-tishoo, a-tishoo,
We all fall down.

It is believed that the "Ring of Roses" refers to the red sores of inflamed carbuncles which appeared after the glandular swellings of the plague.

The Great Plague of 1665 was the last major outbreak of bubonic plague in Britain. Perhaps the Great Fire of London the following year, 1666, played its part in

that it was a killer. As the disease spread, London ceased to function as a city. Some people fled by boat on the River Thames or travelled along the roads. Others shut themselves up in their homes, hoping the plague would not enter there. They did not realize that they were shutting themselves in with the black rats carrying the fleas which were the cause of the disease.

People who did venture out of doors, even if they did not live in London, would carry a pomander, in order to ward off disease. Rich people had elaborate gold or silver pomanders, with many holes through which the sweet-

▲
14 The Queen, the Duke of Edinburgh and the priest all carry posies of flowers at a Maundy Thursday Service. This custom dates back three hundred years. It was originally thought that the scent of flowers kept diseases away.

stamping out the disease. Fire raged across the capital, destroying all the wooden houses and buildings in its path, together with the flea-ridden rats, as the flames spread from Pudding Lane to Pie Corner.

3
A Great Breakthrough

During the Middle Ages there were few skilled surgeons or medical men with any training.

One of the earliest English surgeons was John of Arderne (1306-90). He was an army surgeon who, having served in the Hundred Years War, wrote about his surgical work. The army provided much experience for surgeons, since there were many battle casualties to treat.

Barber-surgeons and Stone-cutters

Among the civilian population, it was the barber-surgeons and stone-cutters who performed surgery. In surgery (or 'chirurgery' as it was formerly called), the patient is cut in order that diseased parts of the body may be removed or any obstruction taken away, whereas a physician uses medicine to effect a cure.

The barber-surgeons, in addition to shaving gentlemen's beards, drew teeth and bled people. It was thought that, by draining a certain amount of blood from a sick person, badness would drain away and the blood would be left "sweet and fine". In reality, this practice weakened anyone who was ill, and made them less able to fight the sickness from which they were suffering.

It was a major operation to have a stone removed by the stone-cutter. There was the danger that organs not connected with the operation would be damaged. All operations were extremely painful. There were no anaesthetics to numb the body. The patient's senses could only be dulled by making him drunk or by giving drugs such as opium. Often the patient did not recover from the operation. It was quite likely that he would bleed to death, or die from infection or shock.

Samuel Pepys

The famous diarist, Samuel Pepys (1633-1703), suffered greatly from a stone which had passed from the kidney to the bladder. The trouble first occurred when he was a student at Cambridge University. Five years later the pain became more frequent. Thomas Hollier, a surgeon at St Thomas's Hospital and an expert stone-cutter, was consulted. Pepys agreed to undergo an operation, and this was performed at a friend's house on 26 March 1658. Pepys recovered, and proudly kept the 56g (2 oz) stone which had been removed. Pepys was always thankful for his return to good health. He knew only too well that this kind of operation frequently resulted in death. In gratitude, Pepys resolved to hold a celebration dinner on each anniversary of the operation.

Schools, Companies and Societies

In Scotland, the Edinburgh School of Surgery was formed in 1505. The surgeons and the barbers joined together to request the Edinburgh Council to allow them to dissect the

5 William Hogarth (1697-1767) painted this picture called "Night". Through the open window, the barber is seen using a cut-throat razor to shave a customer. The striped red and white pole which sticks out prominently above the shop indicates that he is a barber-surgeon. The red represents the blood of a patient, while the white stripes are the bandage which is wound around an injury. One nearby sign shows the bowl into which blood flows during blood-letting, while another sign indicates that the barber-surgeon also draws teeth. From a window above, a chamber pot is indiscriminately emptied into the street – a common, unhygienic practice of the time.

dead bodies of criminals in order to further the knowledge of anatomy. At this time the study of the human body by dissection had hardly begun.

It was not until 1540 that the English Company of Barber-surgeons was granted a charter, although it had been formed in 1461 by Edward IV.

Medical Practitioners

From the sixteenth century rules began to be made to which all who wished to train as a doctor or pharmacist had to conform. A pharmacist mixes and prepares medicine. The old name for this profession is apothecary, and this is still the legal name.

Between the thirteenth and the fifteenth centuries, many universities were founded. Some of these had medical schools, and provision for the sick was provided. Here the patients were "cured". The word originally meant "cared for", but, as a result of this care, many completely recovered from their complaints.

For centuries the only recognized doctor was the physician. He treated the sick with medicine, or, to give it its other name, physic. In earlier centuries the physician did not wish to be connected in any way with the surgeon. The surgeon's work was painful to the patient, often crude and frequently unsuccessful.

Although there had been some great scholars of medicine, including Hippocrates,

very little was known about either surgery or medicine.

The physicians were the thinkers, the observers and the recorders. They were well aware of the deception of the quacks and some untrained practitioners. These learned men began to band together to protect the profession of medicine.

Thomas Linacre

Thomas Linacre (1460-1524) brought together a group of trained physicians. Linacre studied at Oxford and, like him, these men were university graduates. Linacre held the post of Court Physician to Henry VIII and, in 1518, persuaded the monarch to grant a charter to his organization. It was named the Royal College of Physicians of London and given authority to examine and license physicians.

A Royal College of Surgeons was not founded in London until much later. In 1745, the surgeons ceased their association with the barbers and formed the Surgeons' Company. This later became the Royal College of Surgeons of England.

William Harvey

One man who became a Fellow of the Royal College of Physicians made a revolutionary discovery which enabled medical men to understand part of the working of the human body very much better. William Harvey (1578-1650) studied at Cambridge University. He then went to the University of Padua, in northern Italy, which, at that time, was a world-renowned training centre for medicine. It was there that he became interested in the system by which blood is distributed in the body.

On returning to England, Harvey practised as a doctor, and, after a few years, became physician at St Bartholomew's Hospital, London. He also continued his research concerning the human heart and blood. His experiments revealed the direction in which blood flows along veins and arteries.

In 1616, when he gave the Lumleian Lecture to the Royal College of Physicians, Harvey spoke of his findings, and stated: "The movement of the blood is constantly in a circle and is brought about by the beat of the heart."

Harvey continued to find out more about the way blood flowed round the human body. Although he was breaking the law, he returned secretly at night on different occasions to examine the bodies of patients who had died at the hospital. He removed the heart from each corpse and examined it. Eventually he learned what he needed to know – the human heart was a pump.

Harvey discovered the way in which blood is pumped round the body. He was not sure about

16   William Harvey (1578-1650) discovered that blood circulates around the body by means of the pumping action of the heart.

▼

Gutielmus · Harvey · M ·D·

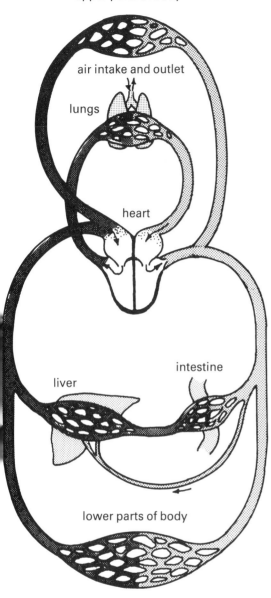

upper parts of body

air intake and outlet

lungs

heart

intestine

liver

lower parts of body

◄ **17** This simplified diagram shows William Harvey's discovery of the way in which blood was pumped by the heart and circulated all over the body.

In 1628 William Harvey published, in Latin, his findings on the circulation of the blood. It was a revolutionary statement. It proved wrong those medical men who thought the heart was a warming device to heat the blood. This and other incorrect beliefs which had been held for centuries had now to be abandoned.

Some people in authority at first refused to acknowledge Harvey's findings, but later his explanations were generally accepted. In medical science, his work became the basis of modern physiology.

Each year an oration called the "Harveian Oration" is given in his honour at the Royal College of Physicians.

The Royal Society

Four Oxford scientists, with Robert Boyle (1627-91) as their leader, succeeded in taking Harvey's discoveries a stage further. Harvey was able to show how the blood circulated. The Oxford scientists discovered *why* blood circulated in this way. They were convinced that the way to discover truth was by careful experimenting and observation, not only of humans but of nature as well.

By 1645, other scientific men had joined the group and The Society of London for Improving Natural Knowledge was founded. In 1662, King Charles II granted a charter enabling the society to prefix the word "Royal" before its name. The title is usually shortened to "The Royal Society".

The aim was to discover as much as possible by the accurate study of nature. Robert Boyle was one of the Society's founders, as was Christopher Wren (1632-1723). Only the most outstanding scientists are made Fellows. They are proud to put the letters F.R.S. after their names. Today, women as well as men can become Fellows of the Royal Society.

he joining of arteries and veins. He guessed that they were connected by what we now call capillaries, but he could see nothing with the naked eye. It was only when the microscope was invented that, in 1661 (after Harvey's death), Marcello Malpighi, an Italian, saw capillaries through the instrument and proved that Harvey was right.

The Study of Anatomy

The forming of the Royal Society was the first step in Britain to combine medicine and science. Medical men studied the habits of wild life. They dissected animals and other creatures to learn about the working of their bodies. So began the serious study of anatomy.

But a stage was reached when the investigators needed to study the internal organs of humans more and more.

It was true that Henry VIII had, in 1540, allowed the bodies of four humans to be used by medical men for the study of anatomy. In 1565, Elizabeth I increased the number by allowing some executed criminals to be dissected.

It was not enough. Surgeons resorted to unlawful methods in order to study what they needed to discover. Even in the eighteenth century, disreputable-looking characters would knock on the rear doors of surgeons houses when darkness had fallen. These were the "resurrection men" who secretly obtained bodies from new graves, or from almshouses or elsewhere before burial could take place. As the body was dragged into the house, the ruffians would put out their hands and receive payment for the job they had done. The surgeon would begin at once to prepare the body for dissection. Only a rope burn around the neck of the victim would reveal that a criminal had met his death by hanging. A few days later, when the medical man had done as much study as he could on the organs of the corpse, the resurrection men – the grave robbers – would again appear late at night, remove the body and take it to bury it in an unmarked grave.

It was a practice that was very much against the law, but it was the only way a medical man could, at that time, discover the knowledge he needed in order to treat people who were sick.

18 Crowds gather to watch the macabre sight of a public hanging. It would appear that, while one dead body is removed by cart, the surgeons at the bottom right hand corner of the platform have already begun removing the internal organs of another victim.

▼

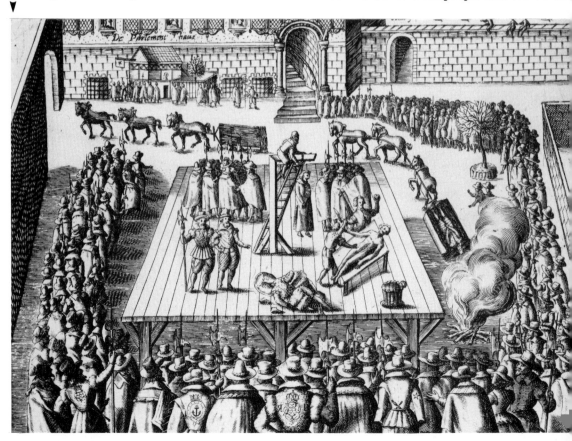

4
Experiment and Epidemic

observant men other than trained physicians and surgeons made medical discoveries. Sir James Lancaster (1554/5-1618), a well-known navigator, was, among other things, in command of the East India Company's fleet which first visited the East Indies. Like other sea-going men, he knew that the crew of any ship would suffer the disease called scurvy. When affected by scurvy, the men became weak, their gums swelled and their faces became yellow, while painful bleeding occurred beneath the body skin. They were not strong enough to carry out the heavy duties required of a sailor on board a wooden, masted ship. Sir James Lancaster discovered that his crew did not suffer from scurvy if they ate plenty of fruit or drank fruit juice. Even when far from any port of call, he tried to make sure there was fruit on board, although he didn't know why it prevented scurvy.

The English Hippocrates

Thomas Sydenham (1624-89) was for some time a trooper in Cromwell's army, but he is remembered as being an outstanding physician. At a time when medical experiments were increasing, Sydenham returned to the methods of Hippocrates. He gained knowledge by what he saw and experienced. He taught his students to observe and study illnesses by watching at the patient's bedside, noting how the illness developed. His treatment of disease was not outlandish, and he used simple remedies wherever possible. One way in which he furthered the progress of medicine was by recording symptoms which enabled the speedy recognition of different fevers and other illnesses.

Sydenham was quickly recognized as an outstanding teacher. Throughout England and Europe he was known as the English Hippocrates. His influence in medicine lasted many years.

Other medical men concentrated on experimenting. The middle of the seventeenth century was a great age of scientific discovery, and science was beginning to influence the art of medicine.

Robert Boyle

Robert Boyle (1627-91) furthered Harvey's work and was a founder of the Royal Society. Boyle was not a physician but a scientist. He is most famous for the scientific law of physics which bears his name – Boyle's Law. Together with his colleagues, Boyle revealed that air is vital to life.

He was the first person in Britain to make a sealed-in thermometer. This enabled the blood heat of humans to be measured. By using this, the physicians found that man's blood was warmer than they had realized. It was also observed that blood temperature is always

Robert Boyle (1621-91) was an outstanding scientist who, by his research and inventions, did much to help medical men understand the human body.

...e same, except when one is ill. Even today, ...e thermometer helps doctors to judge the ...verity of a fever and chart the progress of the ...tient's illness by noting the temperature ...adings shown.

Oxygen

...contemporary of Boyle, Robert Hooke (1635-...'03), one of the founders of the Royal Society, ...as its first curator of experiments. In 1667, ...ooke proved that something was taken out of ...e air by the lungs and transferred to the ...ood. Although exactly what this was was not ...en known, Hooke proved it to be essential to ...e body in order that man could live.
It was not until 1774 that another scientist, ...seph Priestley (1733-1804) isolated this gas.

About 1865, long after Robert Boyle lived, William ...ken introduced this clinical thermometer and ...commended doctors to use it.

It was called oxygen. Its importance in breathing was recognized, and its use in medical treatment is now very important.

Microscopes

In addition to his work on air, Robert Hooke was one of the pioneers in the development of the microscope. The use of lenses had gradually evolved over the years. Lenses were ground to make magnifying glasses. It was a Dutchman, Anton Van Leeuwenhoek (1632-1723) who made one of the first microscopes, but it was very different from the microscopes used today. Leeuwenhoek trapped a single lens between two metal plates and held it to his eye to view the tiny objects he wished to see magnified. He was skilful in making lenses which gave an accurate magnification, and his microscope was very successful.

Robert Hooke went a stage further. He used two lenses, fixed to each end of an adjustable tube. The inner part of the double tube would slide in and out. Hooke was able to draw this out and, by doing so, focus the lenses. It was a great step forward.

Hooke was able to observe tiny insects and other specimens of nature, but sometimes the

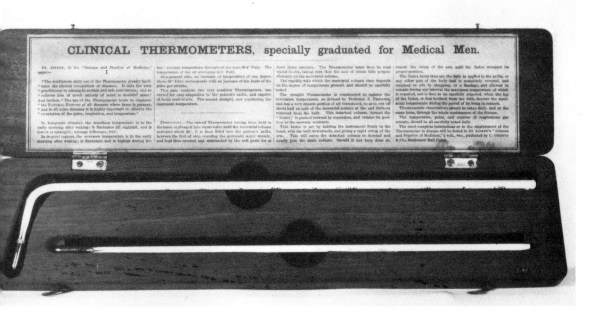

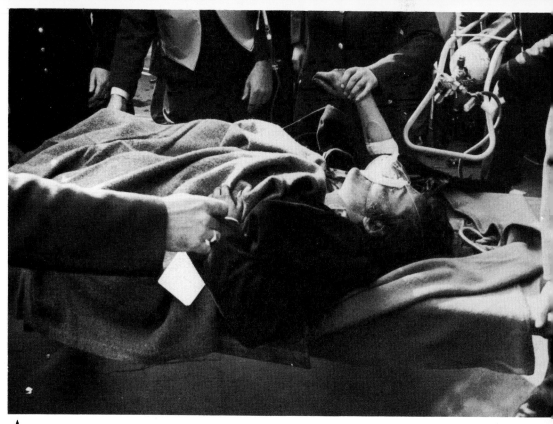

▲

21 Since Robert Hooke (1635-1703) made his discovery in 1667 regarding the use of oxygen by the human body, much more has been learned about the part it can play in medical practice. This casualty in a railway accident which occurred at Moorgate Station, London, in 1975, is given oxygen before being transferred to hospital.

22 The microscope of Robert Hooke (1635-1703) The water-filled glass globe on the left, when plac so that it transmits light, enables a much clearer magnification to be obtained.

▼

view was dim. He found that he could get a clearer magnification if the microscope was placed in bright daylight. This led him to use a glass globe containing water, placed so that it reflected brilliant sunshine onto the specimen under the microscope. It was successful, and Hooke went on to invent a special lamp which could be used at night-time.

Very tiny objects as small as a flea could be seen greatly enlarged and, because of this, the type of microscope became known as a flea glass.

Doctors as well as scientists were now able to observe and study things too small to be seen by the human eye. Ever since the time of

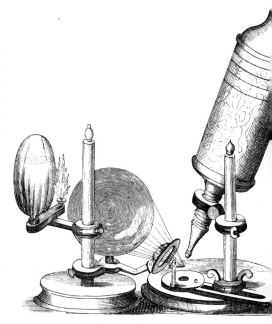

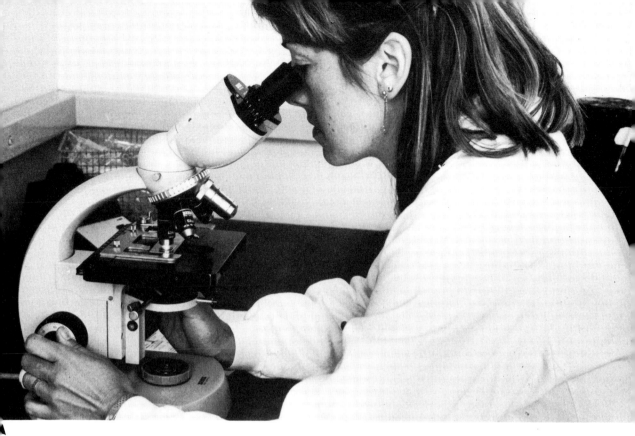

23 A modern microscope is far more complex than Robert Hooke's.

24 This picture shows that the twentieth-century microscope has magnified the pneumococcus (a germ in pneumonia) 1,000 times larger than it actually is.

▼

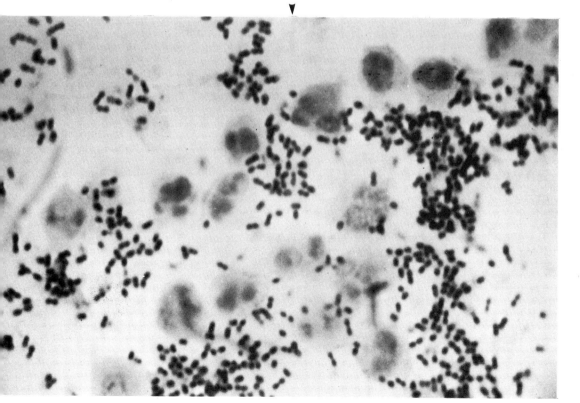

Robert Hooke the microscope has been used by medical men. Today, the modern version of Hooke's microscope plays a major part in the study of disease and the defeat of illness.

Blood Transfusion

Other scientists were carrying out experiments during the same period as Robert Hooke. Another member of the group of scientists led by Robert Boyle was Richard Lower (1631-91), who was also a founder member of the Royal Society.

In 1665, Lower successfully made the first transfusion of blood. It was not between humans, but between dogs.

Centuries passed before, in 1900, a Viennese named Karl Landsteiner discovered that human blood is in four different groups. Only blood from the same group can be successfully transfused from one person to another. Blood banks are now held in Britain and all over the world. A person who has lost a large amount of blood can have it replaced with that of the same blood group.

Smallpox

Despite these moves forward in knowledge and invention, it was not possible to prevent or control an epidemic.

In 1666, a serious outbreak of smallpox swept through Britain. It did not abate until about 1675. For more than 100 years after this, periodic outbreaks of smallpox occurred, some of them reaching serious proportions.

This dreaded disease attacked young and old, rich and poor alike. A fever heralded the onset of the illness. This was followed by a rash which turned into blisters containing pus. When these blisters dried and healed, they left deep scars called pock-marks.

Many did not recover from the illness and the death rate, particularly among children, was high. Those people who did survive rarely had smallpox again.

Most survivors were permanently disfigured by ugly pock-marks. At the monarch's court, ladies were regarded a beauties if their faces were not pitted with pock-marks. Some of the survivors had even worse afflictions. In addition to their look being spoiled, many were left blind, deaf o crippled.

People lived in fear of catching smallpox which spread very quickly. Efforts to comba the disease were made from time to time. On of these attempts was by Lady Mary Wortley Montagu in about 1717. Lady Mary wa married to the British Ambassador to th Turkish Court. While in Turkey, Lady Mary was alarmed to see women inserting smallpox pus into scratches which had been made on the arms of small children.

On enquiry, she found that this was a common practice in Turkey. Assurances were given that the children suffered only a mild form of smallpox and were then protected from having it again. There was no danger of them becoming blind, deaf or crippled, and Lady Mary was told that no deaths had resulted from the inoculations. She was convinced that this was the way to control smallpox, and allowed herself and her small son to be inoculated.

On returning to England, Lady Mary campaigned until smallpox inoculation wa introduced into the country. Even the Roya College of Physicians in London gave thei approval. The result was disastrous Inoculation did not work in England as it appeared to do in Turkey. Not only were thos who were smeared with the smallpox pus a risk, but they quickly transferred the diseas to all around them.

Inoculation Stables

In an attempt to control the infection inoculation stables were set up where children were sent to be inoculated against smallpox For some time before they entered the stables children were prepared. They were bled in order, it was thought, to remove bad blood and leave what was left "pure and healthy". The ate a diet which left them near to the point o

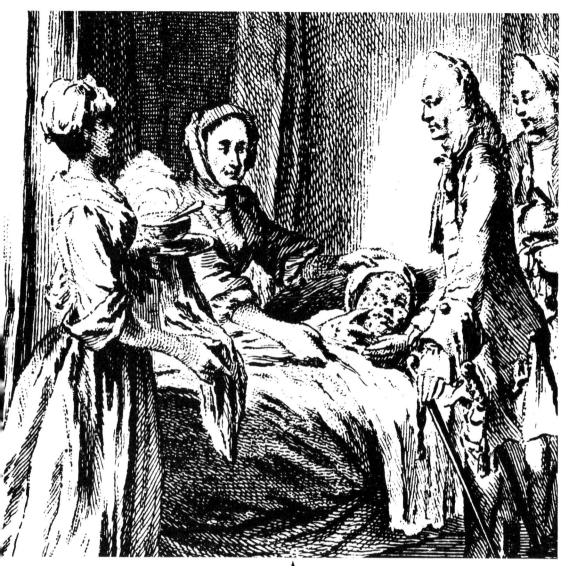

25 This smallpox sufferer's hands and face are covered with blisters. Should he recover, the place where each blister has been will be disfigured by an ugly pock-mark. It is to be hoped that those around him are already protected from the disease. They seem to be completely unaware that they are in danger of catching smallpox themselves.

tarvation. On arrival at the inoculation tables, the parents left and the children were herded together. Often they were tethered to the wall so that, once inoculated, they could not escape and spread smallpox. There was no comfort, the food was poor and the conditions were dirty. When the inoculation period was over, the children were judged to be immune from smallpox and allowed to return home. In reality, they were sickly and weak, and very often suffered some of the nasty effects of smallpox itself.

Despite all this, periodic outbreaks of smallpox occurred among the population, and people still lived in dread of this scourge of man.

5
Smallpox
is Conquered

Edward Jenner (1749-1823) was the man who was eventually responsible for finding out how to overcome smallpox. There were many who went before him who, although they never did any work on smallpox, prepared the way by their dedicated medical study. Their knowledge was handed down one to another until it reached Jenner. The list reads almost like a genealogical tree.

Progress in Scotland

There was much activity in Scottish medical circles. When Sir Robert Sibbald (1641-1722) completed his studies at Leyden University in Holland, he returned to Edinburgh and eventually became the first Professor of Medicine there. In 1681 he founded the Royal College of Physicians of Edinburgh.

Sir Archibald Pitcairn (1652-1713), also a Scotsman, was Professor of Medicine at Leyden University, though not while Sibbald was a student. One of Pitcairn's pupils, Hermann Boerhaave (1668-1738), a Dutchman, was to become a great medical teacher. Boerhaave taught his pupils to learn from the diseases and illnesses they treated, rather than merely listening to lectures or reading books. A number of Scotsmen studied

under Boerhaave and became brilliant physicians.

The Monro Dynasty

One pupil of Boerhaave's, John Monro, was fired with the ambition to make Edinburgh the greatest medical education centre of the

26 The three Alexander Monros – father, son and ▶ grandson.

world. John Monro's son (1697-1767), grandson (1733-1817) and great-grandson (1773-1857) were all named Alexander. The three Alexanders all received the best possible medical training, and each in turn became a professor at the University of Edinburgh.

John Monro's dream came true when, with the opening of an infirmary in 1741, the University of Edinburgh Medical School became a renowned centre of medical learning.

ALEXANDER MONRO, M.D. *F.R.S.*

Lectures in English

Edinburgh carefully trained students, many of whom became specialist medical doctors. When they left the university, they took their knowledge and their skill to many parts of the country and the world.

One of the pupils of the first Alexander Monro was William Cullen (1710-90). Cullen became a professor at both Edinburgh and Glasgow universities and founded the Glasgow Medical School. He was also one of the first professors to lecture in English. Latin had previously been the language used to address university students.

William and John Hunter

William Hunter (1718-83), who came from East Kilbride, was one of Cullen's most famous pupils. In 1770, he set up a School of Anatomy

in Great Windmill Street, London. Not only did he teach, but he collected a large number of anatomical specimens, and these are now kept in the Hunterian Museum at the University of Glasgow.

When William's younger brother, John (1728-93), was twenty years old, he joined William in London. It was only then that John began to study medicine. He soon acquired sufficient knowledge and skill in anatomy and dissection to be able to supervise William' pupils.

John Hunter studied nature. He dissecte animals, birds and insects, and showed ho disease had affected some of the specimens. H assembled an enormous collection c specimens of all sizes and kinds. After Joh Hunter's death, the 13,000 items wer displayed at the premises of the Royal Colleg of Surgeons of England. Unfortunately, part c the collection was destroyed when th buildings were bombed during World War II.

John Hunter showed that anatomy was no

27 The entrance to the University of Edinburgh Medical School.

▼

in itself, a sufficient study on which to base surgery. He stressed the need to consider pathology – the causes, the nature and the remedies of a disease.

In founding surgical pathology, John Hunter raised the status of surgery from a craft which could be unpredictable, to a science needing serious study. The physicians and the surgeons were moving nearer together in their attempt to conquer disease.

Jenner and Smallpox

John Hunter's name became famous, as did that of one particular pupil of his. Edward Jenner (1749-1823) spent two years with John Hunter as his assistant, and they became lifelong friends.

Before going to John Hunter, Jenner, as was normal at that time, served a seven-year apprenticeship under a surgeon. Edward Jenner was only thirteen years old when he went to learn surgery from Daniel Ludlow.

It was during this training that Jenner accompanied Mr Ludlow to a suspected case of smallpox. The surgeon was anxious to know if

28 John Hunter (1728-93) was the first to practise surgical pathology. His work made surgery a science instead of a haphazard practice.

29 John Hunter could never have imagined that his work would lead to the development of a modern hospital laboratory such as this.
▼

30 This portrait of Edward Jenner (1749-1823) is by James Northcote. The artist is careful to include in the picture a copy of Jenner's publication on vaccination.

Edward had been inoculated against the disease. Edward confirmed that he had. He remembered the inoculation stables where he had been left as an eight-year-old only too well. He still experienced the noises in his head which the inoculation left as an aftermath.

It was on this occasion that the alert Edward heard the reply of the milkmaid who, when asked to nurse the smallpox patient, assured Mr Ludlow: "I cannot take the smallpox for I have already had the cowpox." Jenner remembered her words years later.

At the age of twenty, Jenner went to London John Hunter's assistant and student. nner was very successful. He also shared unter's keenness in the study of nature.

Once it was known vaccination was a protection ainst smallpox, people were eager to take vantage of Jenner's discovery. Here, a doctor in the st End of London vaccinates patients of all ages.

At the end of two years, Jenner returned to Berkeley where he lived as a child, and set up his practice as a doctor. He also directed his energies to the study of smallpox. He remembered the milkmaid's words. Jenner knew that the theory about cowpox preventing smallpox was regarded as folklore by the medical profession. "Mere superstition!" the doctors said.

Edward Jenner wondered. In cowpox, the udders of the cow become inflamed and blisters containing fluid are formed. If anyone milks an infected cow and has the slightest scratch or crack in the skin of the hand, it is likely that cowpox will be transmitted to them. An attack is only mild, and soon clears up. But would an attack of cowpox prevent a person from catching smallpox?

Jenner came to believe that, by introducing cowpox pus to the body, a person would be protected against smallpox. After much study and research, he was eventually able to test his theories.

In 1796, Jenner was put in touch with Sarah Nelmes, a milkmaid who was suffering from cowpox. He had already been approached by the mother of eight-year-old James Phipps, with a plea that he should protect the boy from smallpox. And so Jenner transferred the cowpox pus from the hand of Sarah to a scratch he made in the arm of James.

Jenner called the operation "vaccination" because, in Latin, the word "vacca" means "cow". Jenner tested and checked. Sometime after vaccinating James, Jenner inoculated the boy with smallpox pus and James did not develop the disease. The experiment was successful.

Jenner had found a safe way to prevent smallpox, but he met enormous opposition. The medical profession was sceptical. Dr William Woodville of the Smallpox Hospital in London was very antagonistic. The only way that Jenner could have his findings published was at his own expense.

Very, very slowly the practice of vaccination began to be accepted. Gradually its success spread throughout the world. Jenner was honoured in many countries. Smallpox was at first controlled and eventually overcome.

In 1979, two centuries after Jenner lived, the World Health Organisation announced that smallpox had been wiped out.

The Industrial Revolution

While Jenner was quietly and patiently

pursuing his work in the countryside Berkeley, many parts of Britain were bein transformed by the Industrial Revolution.

The change began about 1750. Towns gre rapidly as, in addition to an increase i population, people from the countryside wer

drawn to work in the newly-mechanized mills and factories. Houses were quickly built to provide shelter for the hordes of people transferring to areas where work was available. Most of the buildings were tiny back-to-back houses which were little more

32 Many back-to-back houses like these were built in Liverpool and other towns to house families during the Industrial Revolution. The toilets were not in the tiny houses, but outside in the yard. No wonder disease and ill-health were prevalent in these very cramped conditions.

39

than hovels. They were packed with far more people than they could comfortably accommodate. Sanitary arrangements were poor and the water supply frequently contaminated. The situation was one in which disease spread rapidly.

Typhus, Typhoid and Cholera

Two of the dread diseases were typhus and typhoid. Typhus is caused by the body louse which lives on human blood, while typhoid is carried by food and water supplies which are contaminated by excrement. It was not until the late nineteenth century that doctors realized the different causes of the two illnesses. Since the symptoms of both are the same, it was assumed that they were variations of one disease. Another disease caused, like typhoid, by polluted water supplies, is cholera. All three diseases are killers, and little was known about their treatment or how to control them. It was not until 1854 that Dr John Snow (1813-58) of Westminster traced an outbreak of cholera in the surrounding area to a water pump in Broad Street. The residents living nearby used the pump for their water supply. Dr Snow found that the water had been contaminated by sewage from the house of someone suffering from cholera.

At last it was realized that hygiene played an important part in the prevention of disease. One of the leaders of the movement towards sanitary reform was Edwin Chadwick (1801-90). Chadwick studied law, but was alarmed when he realized the filthy conditions in which the poor people of London lived. As a result of his efforts, a major plan to improve sanitation and provide pure water supplies was begun.

Medical Treatment

Those people who, during the Industrial Revolution, left the country to live in the towns, faced difficulties when they were ill. No longer were they able to go into gardens and fields and pick plants and herbs which had healing properties. The working hours were long; there was no time to prepare home cures.

Because of this, commercially marketed remedies became available. The worker received low wages, and, except in cases of severe illness, could not afford to take time off work or pay to consult a doctor. They were, however, prepared to purchase powders, liniments, tablets and other patent medicines and use them in the hope that their ailment would be relieved.

Tuberculosis

Quite often, though, the disease from which the overcrowded working class population of the Industrial Revolution suffered was, at that time, beyond cure either by pill or physician. The more well-to-do people were not spared either. The biggest killer was tuberculosis. It was also called consumption, since tubercle bacilli which invaded the tissues or organs consumed the affected part of the body.

It was found that the best chance of recovery from the disease was by living in the open air. When the patient was well enough to digest it, he or she was then fed on good, nourishing food.

The patient was not normally treated at home – the risk of spreading the disease was too great. Special open-air hospitals were built in areas well away from the smoke-filled skies and cramped living conditions of the industrial towns. Sometimes these were groups of chalet-like huts which, while open to the fresh air, sheltered the patient from strong winds and stormy weather. Other hospitals had wards, one side of which opened out to enable the patients (even those who were confined to bed) to live as much as possible in the fresh air.

In order to prevent the spread of the disease, great precautions were taken to ensure the most hygienic conditions. Rest, diet and gentle exercise were carefully regulated and adjusted as the patient began to recover. It was reckoned that, after a reasonable length of treatment in this way, half to two thirds of the on-severe cases could be cured of the disease.

Today, there are various ways of preventing the spread of tuberculosis. It is now usual for thirteen-year-olds to be immunized against the disease. Mass Radiography Units check those in colleges, factories and other groups from time to time, and all who have suffered and recovered from the disease have periodic check-ups. Tuberculosis can now be cured by special antibiotics, although it may take a year or more before recovery is considered to be complete.

33 People, unwell because of poor living and working conditions, are persuaded to buy patent medicines and so-called cures from street salesmen.

▼

6
Great
Steps Forward

It was in the middle of the nineteenth century that physicians and surgeons began to work together as one profession – the medical profession. Scientists also began to play a more prominent part in conquering disease.

Nitrous Oxide and Ether

Humphry Davy (1778-1829), superintendent of the Pneumatic Institution in Bristol became interested in the work of Joseph Priestley (1733-1804). He was especially concerned with one gas Priestley had isolated in 1772 called nitrous oxide. In 1800, Davy inhaled some of the gas. It tasted sweet and smelled nice. Very quickly after breathing the gas, Davy felt exhilarated and was convulsed with helpless laughter. Nitrous oxide was popularly called laughing gas. Davy experimented on various animals and, after giving them the gas, he found that they all became wildly excited, and then the anaesthetic effect made them completely unconscious. Each animal soon recovered and showed no ill effects. He tested it on some friends with the same result.

Davy was a scientist and not a medical man

◄ **34** Sir Humphry Davy (1778-1829), although a scientist, made possible one of the most important advances in surgery – the ability to make a patient safely unconscious for a short period of time by means of anaesthetic.

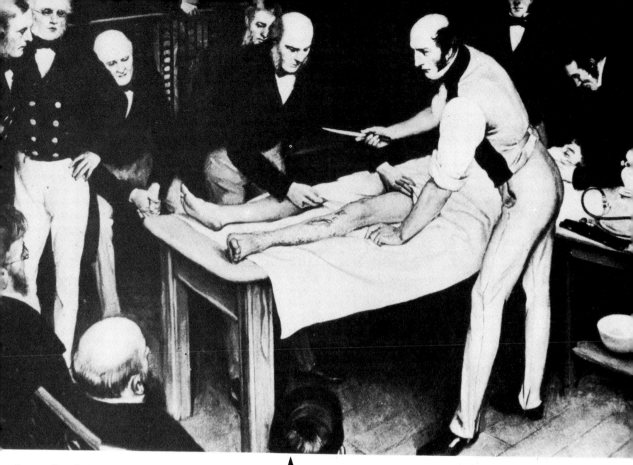

ut he realized the possible use of the gas when umans underwent surgery. Fifteen years fter Davy discovered the anaesthetic roperties of nitrous oxide in 1800, his ssistant Michael Faraday (1791-1867) found nat ether had a similar anaesthetic effect.

In Britain, most medical men showed little nterest. In America, it was different. ttempts were being made to discover omething which would induce harmless eep. In 1846, John Collens Warren (1778-856), a surgeon at Massachusetts General ospital, carried out an operation using ether s an anaesthetic. The patient felt nothing.

In London, Dr Robert Liston (1794-1847) llowed events in America carefully. Liston, a cotsman who received his training and had actised in Edinburgh, was a brilliant rgeon. Liston became Professor of Surgery University College Hospital, London, in 335. He was famed for being able to complete amputation in thirty seconds, thus keeping

35 Dr Robert Liston (1794-1847) about to perform an operation while the patient is under an anaesthetic. This was the first time (1846) that an anaesthetic had been used in Britain during surgery. Joseph Lister (1827-1912) was present on this occasion. He is the young man standing on the left, facing Liston.

the intense pain suffered by the patient to a minimum. Liston was, however, keen to eliminate all pain caused by an operation.

In 1846, Robert Liston used ether as an anaesthetic when he performed an amputation. In was successful and the patient experienced no pain during the operation.

Chloroform

Another Scotsman, James Young Simpson (1811-70), was keenly interested in what was happening. After qualifying at Edinburgh University, it was only eight years before he became Professor of Midwifery there.

43

the chloroform to experience its anaesthet[ic] properties. It was a very foolish thing to d[o] They should have ensured that at least one [of] them did not inhale chloroform. Someo[ne] should have been able to observe the effects [of] the drug on the others and, if necessary, gi[ve] medical assistance. Simpson and the docto[rs] with him were later found unconscious on t[he] floor.

Today, doctors and scientists monitor [their] experiments much more carefully. Safe[ty] regulations, as well as health standards, a[re] very carefully observed by medic[al] practitioners.

After doing more work on chloroforn[m] Simpson knew he had found an acceptab[le] general anaesthetic. It also successful[ly] helped women during childbirth, but Simps[on] met great opposition in using the drug in th[is] way. Many churchmen and some docto[rs] declared that it was against the will of God [to] use an anaesthetic when a child was bor[n]. Opposition was only overcome when Que[en] Victoria requested that chloroform [be] administered to her when she gave birth [to] Prince Leopold in 1853.

Simpson published his findings in 1847 an[d] for the next fifty years chloroform was t[he] most accepted general anaesthetic.

A Local Anaesthetic

Doctors knew that for minor operations it wa[s] not necessary to make the patient complete[ly] unconscious. Alexander Wood (1817-8[?]) realized that an anaesthetic which wou[ld] numb only a small area of the body would n[ot] be inhaled. In 1853, he invented a gla[ss] syringe with a hollow needle, the forerunner [of] the present hypodermic syringe. Wood[’s] needle and syringe would inject an anaesthet[ic] drug into the area of the body needing to b[e] treated. But which drug? Various drug[s] including cocaine, were used, but the searc[h] went on for something better. Success came i[n] 1904, when novocaine was made. It was agree[d] that this was a greatly improved drug for us[e] as a local anaesthetic.

36 Sir James Young Simpson (1811-70), pictured here when he was young. He did further medical work on anaesthetics and found that chloroform was the most suitable.

Simpson wondered about the possibility of using an anaesthetic during childbirth. He considered ether, but found it had its drawbacks: the smell was unpleasant, it irritated the eyes and also caused sickness.

He tried alternatives, but found nothing suitable until chloroform, a drug which had been discovered in 1831, was brought to his notice. Simpson discussed the matter with a group of doctors, and together they all inhaled

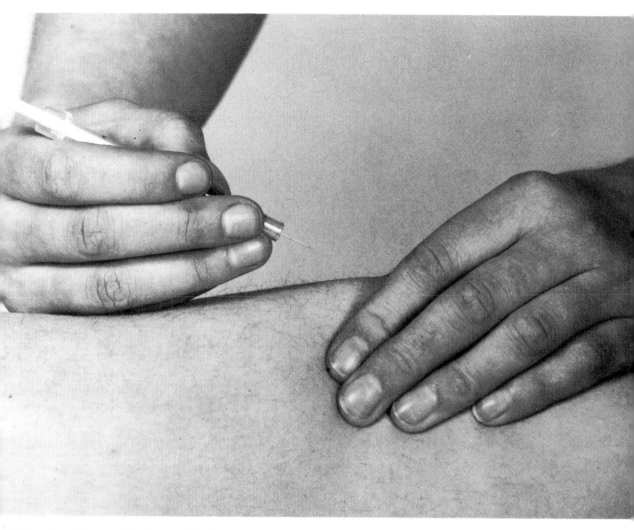

7 A syringe being used to give an injection.

James Syme

Meanwhile, a Scottish surgeon named James Syme (1799-1870) was gaining a reputation throughout Europe as a brilliant surgeon and teacher. He was Professor of Clinical Surgery at Edinburgh University. Although sometimes a controversial figure, it was agreed that no one could surpass him and that "He never wasted a word, a drop of ink or a drop of blood."

When he began his training, James Syme studied under Robert Liston. In 1846, a student of Syme's was present when Liston performed the first operation under anaesthetic in Britain. Syme's young student was Joseph Lister.

Joseph Lister

Lister (1827-1912), who came from Upton in Essex, had studied at University College Hospital, London, before going to Edinburgh for further study. After completing his training, he held the post of Assistant Surgeon

38 Sir Joseph Lister (1827-1912), whose Antiseptic Method made recovery from surgery or illness much more likely. He is pictured here as the President of the Royal Society.

and Lecturer at Edinburgh Royal Infirmary. It was, however, in 1860, when he became Professor of Clinical Surgery at Glasgow, that he began his most important work.

Lister followed the progress of medicine in all parts of the world, and was especially interested in the work of Louis Pasteur in France. Pasteur discovered that germs in the air, so small that the eye could not see them, were causing bacterial action which resulted in events such as the souring of milk or the fermentation of wine.

Joseph Lister was curious. If air-borne germs could affect liquids, he reasoned, could they not also affect open wounds? Lister became convinced that germs were responsible for the high death rate in surgery.

Doctors operated wearing the ordinary suits they wore about the town. Instruments were not washed or sterilized after operating on one patient after another. After examining dead bodies, a doctor went on to attend to his patients. No rules of hygiene or cleanliness were observed. No wonder that, after surgery, the survival rate was low.

Lister began experiments to find something which would prevent germs entering surgical cuts and turning them septic. It came to his notice that carbolic acid was being used to purify sewage at Carlisle. He decided to test it.

Lister soaked everything in the strong carbolic acid, including his own hands, his instruments, bandages and the patient's leg on which he was to operate. The carbolic acid was much too strong. His patient suffered great pain and the flesh was burnt – but there was no poisoning of the wound. Lister used diluted carbolic acid the next time he operated. This did not harm the patient but still prevented any poisoning of the wound. Lister had found an effective antiseptic.

In 1867, Lister published the results of his work in *The Lancet*, the medical journal. As is

39 While the surgeon operates, Lister's Carbolic Spray fills the air with an antiseptic mist, and, at the same time, the patient is unconscious, having been given chloroform.

▼

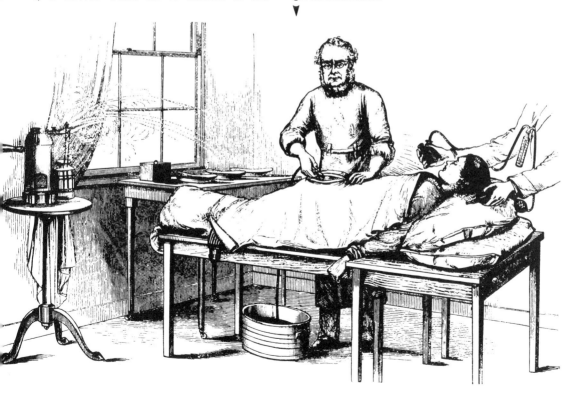

often the case with new discoveries, there were those who disbelieved and criticized Lister's work. In London especially, there was a great deal of antagonism. It took more than ten years before Lister's findings about antiseptic treatment, including cleanliness, were acknowledged throughout the world.

The King is Ill

King Edward VII was suddenly taken ill with appendicitis just before his coronation in June 1902. Although appendicitis is now normally a routine operation, at that time it was very dangerous. Lister was called to Buckingham Palace. He advised that an operation, using antiseptics, should be carried out. This was done and the king rapidly recovered. His coronation took place early in August 1902.

What became known as Lister's Antiseptic Method was accepted by the medical profession and the general population as well. His policy of keeping germs away from a patient and killing those that are there revolutionized surgery and made it much safer.

Sir Ronald Ross

Ronald Ross (1857-1932) trained as a doctor at St Bartholomew's Hospital, London. He worked in India as a member of the Indian Medical Service and was responsible for the health of British soldiers.

Malaria was an illness which was common in India. It had been known for centuries, and in Britain it was called the ague. Since it was thought that the fever was caused by bad air and the Italian words "mala aria" mean "bad air", the disease was eventually called "malaria". No one knew how or why the illness occurred, although it was thought that mosquitoes on misty marshes in hot countries might be the source of the infection.

Ronald Ross was determined to find out. He studied different kinds of mosquito, examining them all carefully under a microscope. Eventually, in 1897, he discovered that the female *Anophales* mosquito was responsible for the infection. Having bitten a person suffering from malaria, this insect then carries the disease to the next healthy person it bites.

Ronald Ross tried to control malaria by destroying the mosquitoes. He was ridiculed to such an extent that caricatures of "Mosquito Ross" appeared in the press. It was twenty years before Ross proved he was right and his work was acknowledged. In his honour, the Ross Institute and Hospital for Tropical Diseases was founded in London. A year after the death of Ronald Ross, it was united with the London School of Hygiene and Tropical Medicine.

Malaria is still a severe illness but quinine and other modern drugs are effective in overcoming it. The powerful insecticide known as DDT has helped to kill off large numbers of mosquitoes.

The work of Sir Ronald Ross is still continued by the World Health Organisation. A campaign to wipe out malaria all over the world was begun in 1955.

The anophales mosquito which carries the disease does not live in northern Europe. Any cases of malaria which occur in Britain are usually due to immigrants and travellers from overseas who have been infected before they arrive. Fortunately, when travelling from Britain to other countries, it is possible to be protected from the illness by taking anti-malarial drugs before commencing the journey.

Sir Ronald Ross did not discover a drug or medicine to cure malaria, but practised preventive medicine in order to control it. Today, preventive medicine is increasingly used. The aim is to keep people healthy and to prevent them from becoming ill, in preference to trying to cure them after they have caught a disease.

40 Sir Ronald Ross (1857-1932), physician and poet. After years of careful work, he discovered that the anophales mosquito carries malaria from an infected person to a healthy one.

7
The Part
Women Played

Until the second half of the nineteenth century women took no part at all in the professional practice of medicine. They were not allowed to. It was not deemed fit that any gentlewoman should study medicine. A woman's place was in the home.

In 1800, the Royal College of Surgeons was founded in London and, thirty-two years later, the British Medical Association was formed. Women, however, were not admitted. For one thing, there were no women doctors. There were many other restrictions.

Some women resented this. They were far-sighted and forward thinking. These highly intelligent women came mainly from well-to-do families. They took action in order to overcome what they believed to be wrong.

Elizabeth Fry

One of these women was Elizabeth Fry (1780-1845). She was a Quaker and at seventeen years of age resolved to dedicate her whole life to the service of God. Even when she was twenty and married Joseph Fry, a banker, her resolve did not diminish. She helped the poor and nursed the sick, and even helped to vaccinate the local children against smallpox.

In 1813, when she was thirty-three, Elizabeth became aware of the plight of women prisoners in Newgate jail. The conditions were deplorable. The dark, badly ventilated cells contained only dirty, damp straw for the inmates to sleep on. Sanitary arrangements were non-existent and disease spread unchecked. Epidemics were commonplace and many prisoners died from "jail fever". "Jail fever" was the term given to a form of typhus fever which occurred in the prisons.

Elizabeth Fry went to Newgate to see for herself. She found 300 women, many of whom had children with them, crushed together in one room. Even the jailers who had reluctantly admitted Elizabeth refused to go among the screaming, fighting women on their own.

Elizabeth insisted on going into the room by herself. Before she could be attacked, she picked up one of the grubby little children. The women watched, and then, as Elizabeth spoke, they listened. Gradually Elizabeth gained the confidence of the women and in a short time was able to embark on the work she intended to do. To begin with, she set up a school in Newgate for young offenders and the children of the prisoners. She arranged for the women to be taught needlework, so that they could make and repair their children's clothes. Later, the women were taught to sew patchwork articles and these, together with stockings knitted by the women, were sold. The money raised was used for the prisoners' benefit.

Elizabeth imposed some rules. Before they began sewing, the women had to be clean and behave quietly. The reform in the prisons was

noticeable. The health of the prisoners improved and disease became less prevalent.

Occupational Therapy

Although Elizabeth Fry did not realize it, she had begun what is now known as occupational therapy. Quite apart from work among prisoners, today it is practised among ordinary sick people. The aim is to help them to lead as normal a life as possible, to have an interest and to do as much for themselves as they can. In this way, recovery is speeded up. Today, occupational therapy includes basket work, painting, needlework and many other activities.

▲
41 Elizabeth Fry (1780-1845) improved the physical and mental condition of women prisoners.

42 Elizabeth Fry is shown reading to women prisoners. The notice on the wall gives a stern warning of the consequences should any of the Bibles or books provided be damaged. Notice the attitudes of the prisoners, and compare them with those of the fashionably dressed visitors on the left.
▼

43 This is an actual photograph of Florence Nightingale (1820-1910).

Florence Nightingale

It was the Crimean War which enabled Florence Nightingale (1820-1910) to bring about reforms which she knew were needed. She might have been considered the person least able to do the job. Her parents were wealthy and it was expected that Florence would lead the life of a lady. Florence was not prepared to accept this. She disturbed her parents by announcing that she would like to become a nurse.

In the nineteenth century nursing was a degrading occupation. No longer did medieval nuns, with gentle and loving care, nurse the sick. In the time of Florence Nightingale nurses were known as dirty, low-living women, who drank alcohol to excess. It was one of the lowest occupations.

Florence insisted, and persuaded her parents to allow her to become a nurse. They stressed that she must receive proper training. Since none was available in Britain, Florence spent several months in France and Germany studying nursing.

On her return to London, Florence became the Matron of "an Establishment for Gentlewomen during Illness" in Harley Street.

The Crimean War

The Crimean War broke out in 1854 and England, France and Turkey combined to

44 This famous picture is an artist's impression of Florence Nightingale. The Lady with the Lamp visited the hospital wards each night, making sure that every injured soldier was comfortable.

▼

fight Russia. The barracks at Scutari, near Constantinople, were used as a hospital. The news came back to England that conditions there were unsatisfactory.

A despatch from war reporter William Russell was printed in *The Times*, and asked: "Are there no devoted women among us able and willing to go forth and minister to the sick and suffering soldiers of the East in the hospitals of Scutari? Are none of the daughters of England at this extreme hour of need ready for such a work of mercy?"

Florence Nightingale was ready. She gathered together thirty-eight volunteers. They left England quickly and arrived in Scutari on 5 November 1854. Just as Elizabeth Fry found in the prisons, Florence Nightingale was confronted in the war hospitals with a lack of hygiene, poor feeding arrangements and other unsanitary conditions which contributed to the spread of infection. Soap and towels were not supplied. Often the men had no clothes other than the army uniforms they had been wearing when they were injured.

Florence Nightingale tried to improve matters, but was opposed by both the military and medical authorities. Only after an epidemic was she allowed to make the changes necessary to raise the standard of cleanliness and general welfare. Two years later, when the war ended, the death rate in the hospitals had dropped from 40% to 2%.

Florence Nightingale also cared for the general welfare of the soldiers as she and her helpers nursed them back to health. By her practice of touring the wards each night after dark to ensure that each man was comfortable, Florence Nightingale earned for herself the title of "The Lady with the Lamp".

Florence Nightingale extended her work. She set up other military hospitals in the Crimea, wrote books about hospitals and nursing, and was one of the founders of the Red Cross Society.

People in England raised £50,000 and gave it to Florence as a thank offering when she returned to Britain. With this money, she founded a training school for nurses at St Thomas's Hospital in London. It was called The Florence Nightingale School and Home for Nurses.

Florence Nightingale was not physically strong, but she did all she could to make nursing a respectable profession. She organized training for nurses which complied with the highest medical standards. The foundations of today's nursing profession were laid by Florence Nightingale.

Elizabeth Garrett Anderson

About the time that Elizabeth Fry's work in reforming the prisons had become accepted world wide, and the young Florence

45 Elizabeth Garrett Anderson (1836-1917) who opened the way for women to become doctors.
▼

Nightingale had resolved to become a nurse, Elizabeth Garrett (1836-1917) was born in London. As a teenager, Elizabeth was sent to boarding school. The headmistress expressed the view that women should be able to lead a fuller life than that which was spent entirely in the home. The idea of greater opportunities for women appealed to Elizabeth, but she could not see how this could come about. After leaving school, she lived at home in the conventional way until she was about twenty-two years old. During this time, she tried to improve her own education, studying Latin and mathematics among other subjects.

While visiting an old school friend, Elizabeth met Elizabeth Blackwell, who was the only woman doctor in the world. After a fight to overcome enormous difficulties, Dr Blackwell had qualified in America. Elizabeth Garrett resolved that she would become the first woman doctor in England.

Mr and Mrs Garrett were very much against the idea, but once her father realized how determined Elizabeth was he supported and helped her all he could.

Since there were no facilities for women to be trained as doctors, Elizabeth began by becoming a nurse at the Middlesex Hospital. She picked up as much medical knowledge as she could and arranged to have private tuition from some of the hospital's doctors.

Difficulties and obstacles were placed in Elizabeth's way, not because she was unable to do the work or pass the examinations, but because she was a woman. Gradually, with the help of her father (who even threatened legal action against the medical authorities), Elizabeth completed the necessary training. She sat the examinations and passed, gaining the Licentiate of the Society of Apothecaries. At the age of twenty-nine, she became the first woman medical practitioner in Britain.

Elizabeth was not content to make her successful medical practice the whole of her work. Many of her patients were women, who were glad to discuss their ailments with another woman. There was no National Health Service at this time. Treatment had to be paid for. Elizabeth was aware that many poor women were unable to afford a doctor's fee. In order to help them, she opened St Mary's Dispensary, and here women and children were treated by Elizabeth Garrett, who charged very little for her services.

Another thing Elizabeth was not content with was her qualification. The Licentiate of the Society of Apothecaries permitted her to dispense and practise medicine. Most male practitioners held a degree enabling them to use the title "Doctor". With her usual determination, Elizabeth found out how she could become Doctor Garrett. Since women were not admitted to courses in Britain, she enrolled at the University of the Sorbonne in Paris, where, not long before, it had been agreed to admit women.

In 1870, Elizabeth Garrett was examined by the University. She passed each of the six required subjects with distinction, even though the whole of the proceedings were in French.

She was now Doctor Elizabeth Garrett. No longer could the British medical profession regard her as inferior.

Shortly afterwards, Elizabeth married James Anderson, a shipowner. It was agreed that Elizabeth should continue her work, and she became known as Dr Elizabeth Garrett Anderson.

Elizabeth joined the council of the newly-formed training centre called the London School of Medicine for Women. Difficulties arose because medical boards refused to examine candidates from the school. Dr Garrett Anderson joined a deputation seeking government legislation which required that women should be examined by the British medical examining boards. This resulted in the Medical Act of 1876. At last, women medical students were accepted by the profession.

From then on, Elizabeth Garrett Anderson held posts of increasing importance. She died in 1917. Shortly afterwards, St Mary's Dispensary, which had been enlarged and re-named The New Hospital for Women, was given another title. It was called The Elizabeth Garrett Anderson Hospital. This hospital, staffed by women, still treats women today. For a time, it seemed as if it would have to close, but, once more, the work is expanding. In March, 1984, new outpatients' accommodation, an operating theatre and a twenty-bed ward opened to receive women patients. An Early Diagnosis Unit is planned.

Elizabeth Garrett Anderson made the way possible for intelligent and educated women to study, qualify and practise the profession of medicine.

46 The new buildings of the Elizabeth Garrett Anderson Hospital for Women, which were opened in March, 1984.
▼

8
Modern Drugs and Diseases

Sir Frederick Gowland Hopkins

In the nineteenth century several diseases were prevalent for which there was no known cure. Children whose leg bones were curved instead of straight suffered from rickets, Eastern races were anaemic and paralysed because of a disease called beri-beri, and scurvy was still a serious problem among sailors. Although Sir James Lancaster (1554/5-1618) had realized that fresh fruit could prevent scurvy, no-one had discovered why it had this effect. Different scientists tried to solve the problem. One of these was Sir Frederick Gowland Hopkins (1861-1947). In 1912, Hopkins found that these illnesses were suffered when vital parts of food were missing in the diet, especially if the food was not fresh or was wrongly cooked. These tiny essentials were caled vitamins. People suffered from rickets, beri-beri, scurvy and other complaints when their diet was deficient in vitamins. Illnesses caused by the shortage of vitamins and important food items in the diet became known as "deficiency diseases". They cause malnutrition and affect the mental health of the sufferer.

In the case of vitamin deficiency, Frederick Gowland Hopkins found that health could be restored and illness prevented by including the necessary vitamins in the diet.

There are at least seventeen vitamins which

▲
47 Sir Frederick Gowland Hopkins (1861-1947) in his laboratory. He discovered the necessity to include vitamins in the diet.

prevent different diseases. Vitamins are listed by the letters of the alphabet. It is known that vitamin C in fruit and some vegetables prevents scurvy, and that beri-beri is controlled by vitamin B_1, while vitamin D in dairy produce prevents rickets. Vitamins are not drugs, but are a natural part of the food they are in.

The Influenza Epidemic

Towards the end of World War I, a serious epidemic of influenza spread across the world. It began in Autumn 1918 and continued into the following year. So many people died from this virus disease that its severity was compared with the Black Death. In just one month, the outbreak, which was termed "Spanish 'flu", swept across the northern hemisphere. There were many casualties in Britain. More people in the world died during this epidemic of virus infection than were killed in all the fighting in World War I.

In 1933, research workers succeeded in finding one virus which was the cause of the infection. Various types of the influenza virus have since been isolated, and this gives doctors some lead in overcoming the disease.

In 1947, the World Health Organisation set up a World Influenza Centre in London, in order to find out more and so keep the disease under control.

Penicillin

The reliance on drugs to control and conquer disease has increased enormously during the twentieth century.

In 1906, a young Scot accepted the post of Assistant Bacteriologist at St Mary's Hospital, Paddington. His name was Alexander Fleming (1881-1955). The staff of the Inoculation Department where Fleming worked carried out research and experiments in an attempt to overcome infections of the body. One task was to take specimens from hospital patients and, having placed them on flat glass culture plates called petri dishes, to carry out various tests and experiments, and then study the results.

Fleming's work was interrupted during World War I, but he returned to St Mary's, Paddington, in 1918. He was given more responsible appointments, eventually becoming the Assistant Director of the Inoculation Department and Professor of Bacteriology at London University.

Fleming continued his research. One day he lifted the cover of a petri dish and found that the specimen on it became contaminated by germs in the air. A mould began to grow on the dish and the experiment was spoiled.

Normally, a scientist would discard the specimen and patiently begin again, but Fleming did not. He was known to have keen powers of observation. He looked carefully to see what had happened. He tested further and discovered that the growing mould had destroyed the germs. In other experiments, Fleming was able to transfer the germ-killing properties of the mould into a liquid. He called this penicillin. Alexander Fleming had discovered a powerful killer of germs.

But there were problems. One was that penicillin soon lost its strength. Fleming was a bacteriologist. The problems needed to be solved by a chemist. There was no skilled chemist on the staff of the laboratory available to do the work. Alexander Fleming published his findings, but had to cease work on the project and continue with other research.

Florey and Chain

Fleming discovered penicillin in 1928. It was not until 1937 that two scientists carrying out research at Oxford University read Fleming's reports and became interested. Professor Howard Florey (1898-1968) was born in Australia, and Dr Ernst Boris Chain (1906-79), a chemist, was a refugee from Hitler's

48 Sir Alexander Fleming (1881-1955) at St Mary's ▶ Hospital, Paddington, London. A petri dish, similar to the one on which penicillin first began to grow, is seen near his left hand.

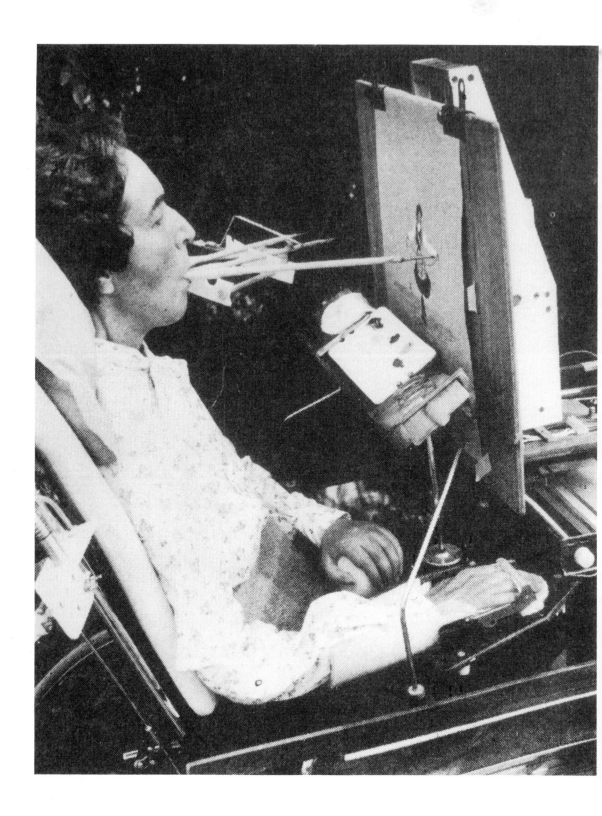

9 Elizabeth Twistington-Higgins, MBE, a former ballet dancer who is almost totally paralysed by polio. She is now a famous artist, painting all her pictures by holding the brush in her mouth.

Germany. Their work progressed, they solved the problems, and by 1941 penicillin was being used to cure humans.

Unfortunately, World War II (1939-45) prevented the manufacture of penicillin in large quantities in Britain and yet the new wonder drug was needed to treat the military and civilian war wounded.

Professor Florey solved the problem by going to America and arranging for penicillin to be manufactured there. Meanwhile, Alexander Fleming convinced the Minister of Supply that penicillin must be produced in England, and production began shortly afterwards. Penicillin saved the lives of many war casualties and has continued to cure sickness ever since.

Other scientists began to discover more germ-killing drugs such as streptomycin and aureomycin. This type of drug is called an antibiotic.

Poliomyelitis

Despite the increasing amount of medical research being carried out, in the late 1940s there was an epidemic of poliomyelitis in Britain. The name is sometime shortened to "polio". It is also called infantile paralysis, although young children are not the only victims of the disease. Those who contract polio often remain paralysed, with different

50 Polio sufferers whose lungs are affected need assistance to help them to breathe. The cumbersome box-type appliance on the left is an iron lung. Apart from the head, it totally enclosed the patient. The lady on the right is using an electronic lung. This is much more convenient, and, once it is connected, can be controlled by the patient without any other assistance.
▼

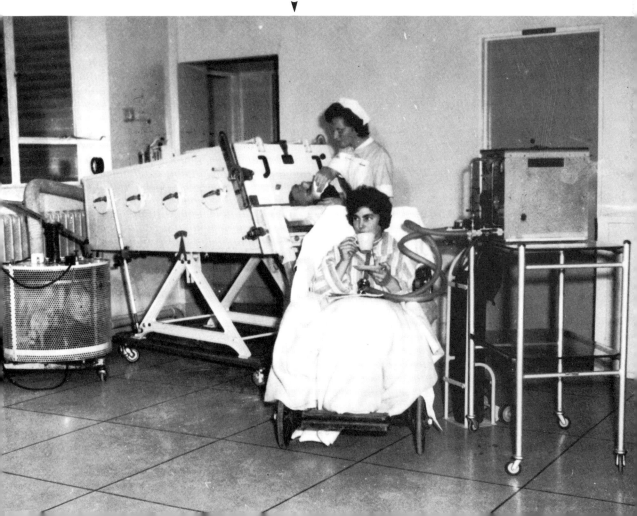

degrees of disability, when the initial attack of fever has passed.

Doctors and scientists increased their efforts to stamp out polio. Dr Jonas Salk (1914-   ), an American, produced a vaccine in 1955 which would prevent poliomyelitis but would not cure it. Two years later, a programme of vaccination began in Britain. Babies and young children were injected with the Salk vaccine in order to prevent them catching polio. Another American vaccine, discovered by Dr Albert Sabin (1906-   ) is taken by the mouth. This has been used in Britain since 1962.

Polio is far less common than it was, although it is still necessary to take measures to prevent it. Like smallpox, it will take years before polio can be completely wiped out.

Today, it is possible to be protected against many diseases, including polio, whooping cough, diphtheria and tuberculosis. A timetable of immunization is carried out from babyhood onwards.

Thalidomide

It is now known that drugs can cause problems as well as healing and relieving suffering. The tragic thalidomide disaster occurred in 1961. Some expectant mothers were prescribed the drug thalidomide during pregnancy. As a result, their babies were born with deformities. Arms and legs were short or non-existent; hands, feet, fingers and toes were under-developed or malformed. Immediately it was proved that thalidomide was the cause of these deformities, the drug was withdrawn.

Those who were deformed because of thalidomide are now young adults. Everything has been done to provide them, and others with similar needs, with artificial limbs which enable them to carry out as many functions as possible. These appliances move into various positions and perform different tasks by means of switches. These switches are controlled by the person wearing the artificial limb. Switches are manipulated by whatever points of the body are able to be used.

Rheumatic Illnesses

Many people, particularly the elderly, suffer from rheumatism and associated complaints. When cortisone was discovered in America in 1949 it seemed as if it was a miracle cure. Sadly, it was found that it caused other ill effects on the human body. More recently, new drugs to combat arthritis and similar ailments have been produced and used, including some British ones. Some, like opren, have proved to be unsatisfactory because they cause serious side effects. While the rheumatic complaint is relieved, these drugs damage other organs of the body.

Research goes on to find drugs and other methods of safely curing and controlling rheumatic illnesses.

◄ **51** This thalidomide victim was born without limbs. She now uses artificial arms and hands to enable her to paint and do many other things.

9
Medicine Today

Cancer

One of the major diseases which doctors and scientists are fighting to overcome is cancer. In this, cells in the body multiply uncontrollably, eventually spreading and damaging different organs. A lot of progress has been made in treating cancer. Research is gradually revealing important facts about body cells and cancerous tissues. It is now known that if cancer is disgnosed and treated early, it is much more likely that the patient will make a full recovery. In addition to surgery, highly technical methods in the diagnosis and treatment of cancer have been devised. These include ultrasound and radio-isotope scanning, radiotherapy and laser beam treatment.

Organ Transplants

Great advances have been made in "spare part" surgery. Organs can now be transplanted from one person to another, although the success rate is, as yet, variable. Kidney transplants now save many lives, and enable patients to receive a kidney from another person to function instead of their own diseased organs. These people are then able to live much more normal lives, instead of having to rely on kidney dialysis. Dialysis is a cumbersome but successful method by which a machine does the work of the kidneys in filtering the blood to cleanse it of poisons.

Heart Diseases

A great breakthrough in transplant surgery took place in 1967. Dr Christiaan Barnard (1922-), in South Africa, performed the first human heart transplant. Since then, the operation has been performed a number of times, with varying degrees of success. In

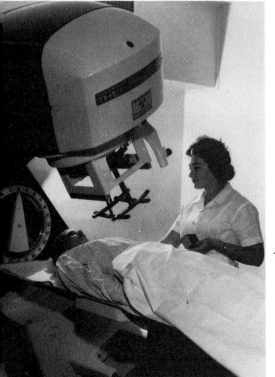

◀ **52** Many kinds of advanced appliances are now used for the diagnosis and treatment of cancer. This teletherapy machine uses radioactive cobalt 60.

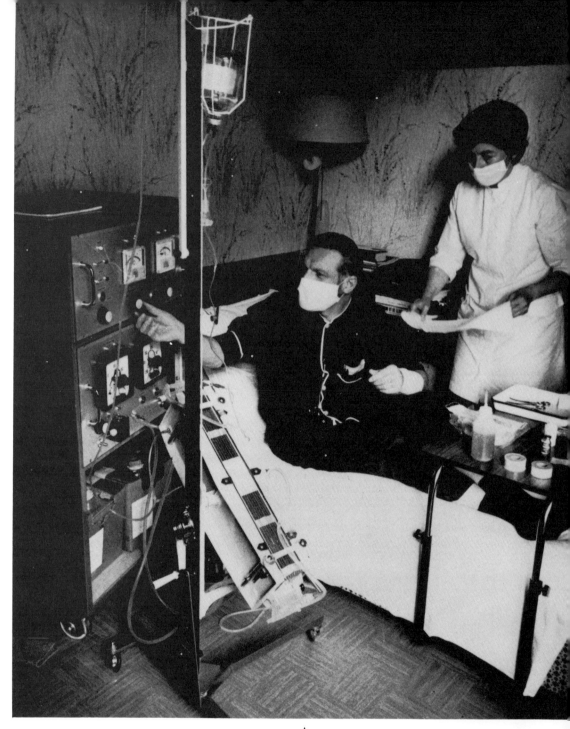

England, Mr T.A.H. English (1932-) at Papworth Hospital, Cambridgeshire, and Mr Magdi Yacoub at Harefield Hospital, Middlesex, have, with their teams, successfully carried out heart transplants.

53 After two months' training in hospital, this kidney patient is able to use the dialysis machine which has been installed in his own home. His wife stands by, ready to help.

Heart disease is very prevalent in the civilized world, although a lot can now be done to prevent and overcome the effects of different heart complaints. Heart transplant is only carried out as a last resort.

Another modern invention which is of benefit to those suffering from certain heart defects is the pacemaker. This tiny instrument is inserted in the patient's chest and attached to the heart. The pacemaker regulates the heart beat and controls it at a desired, steady rate.

Diet

Because of an increase in heart disease, people are being persuaded to give more attention to diet and exercise. Overweight people are encouraged to shed excess weight by controlling the amount and type of food they

54　Mr T.A.H. English, the heart transplant surgeon at Papworth Hospital, Cambridgeshire.

55　Mr Keith Castle, Britain's longest surviving heart transplant patient, whose operation was performed by Mr T.A.H. English in August 1979.

▲
56 Mr Magdi Yacoub, who was born in Egypt, is the leader of the heart transplant team at Harefield Hospital, Middlesex, where many successful operations have been carried out.

58 The diet of those in hospital is carefully planned to help recovery. Here, a hospital dietitian discusses with two patients the meals they will be having.
▼

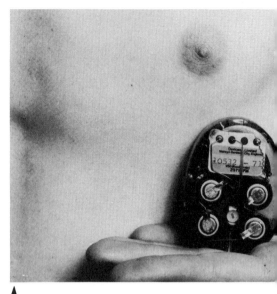

▲
57 This instrument, about the size of a golfball, is the pacemaker which regulates and controls the heart beat of a person with a heart defect. The surgeon performs an operation to insert the pacemaker inside the patient's chest and connects the instrument to the heart.

59 Posters warning of the dangers of smoking are ▶ issued periodically. This one is a reminder that lungs contaminated by smoking cannot be cleaned as easily as dirty hands.

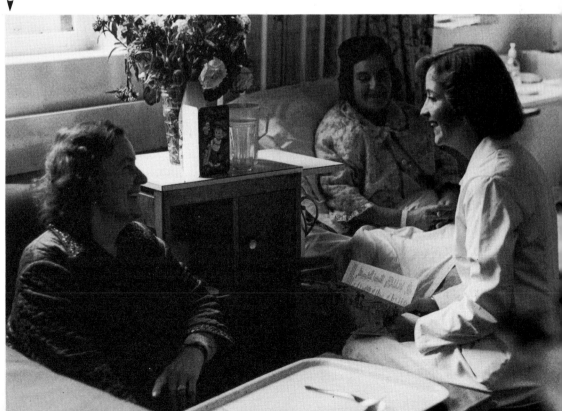

eat. By regaining a healthy weight, the stress on the body, and especially the heart, is relieved.

Good health is also helped by eating more fibre-containing wholefoods such as wholemeal bread, bran, potatoes, fruit and vegetables, and cutting out an excess of fats, sugar and salt. There is also an awareness that chemical additives in food, used to flavour, colour or preserve a product, can cause disease and be harmful to health.

Coupled with diet, various forms of exercise, from gentle to very vigorous, are recommended in order to increase stamina and maintain peak physical fitness.

Preventive Medicine

Preventive medicine is increasingly practised today in various ways. Where immunization is possible, it is encouraged.

Disease can also be prevented by avoiding things that may cause it. The dangers of

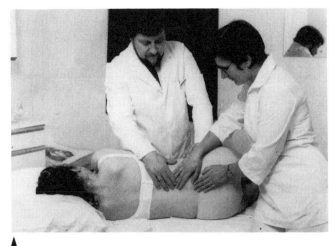

▲ **60** Qualified osteopaths are seen treating a patient suffering from back pain.

tobacco smoking have become well known in recent years. It was clear that smoking aggravated chest ailments such as bronchitis and coughs. Things took a more serious turn when, in 1957, the Medical Research Council warned of a suspected link between smoking and lung cancer. In 1962, a report by the Royal College of Physicians confirmed that cigarette smoking was the most likely cause of many deaths from lung-cancer. It was also suspected that the development of coronary heart disease could be attributed to smoking.

As a result of these findings, in 1962 a big campaign was launched to reduce tobacco smoking and so prevent the serious illnesses caused by it. Further campaigns, including television programmes designed to help people to stop smoking, take place regularly.

Alternative Medicines

Alongside conventional medicine, other treatments are practised. These are termed alternative or fringe medicines and are normally only available to patients who pay. Some treatments, including acupuncture and massage, originated in China many centuries ago. Acupuncture is for the relief of pain and involves the pricking of specific points on the body with fine needles. Those who practise acupuncture believe that pain is caused by a disturbance of the points of the body at which the needles are required to be placed.

ou can't scrub
ur lungs clean.

ng cancer kills ten times more smokers
than non-smokers.

Osteopathy is increasingly being used in this country to treat patients who suffer pain in various joints. Modern treatment by osteopathy uses techniques with electricity, massage and, in some cases, surgery.

Homeopathy is another form of alternative medicine. In this, the theory is that by giving a drug which will produce symptoms of the disease from which the patient is suffering, the body will be stimulated to overcome the disease.

Other alternative medicines are, as yet, practised only by a minority. These include naturopathy, reflexology, the Alexander technique and the Bach flower remedies.

There is a revival in herbalism. Not only are herbs being used for medicinal use, but their inclusion in diet as a way to promote good health is increasing.

Although those who believe in these remedies claim great success in their results, there is no guarantee that they will work. Whereas it is possible for anyone to practise alternative medicine without any qualifications, there are some training centres such as the British School of Osteopathy and the London Homeopathic Hospital. The practice of alternative medicine and any qualification for it is not recognized by the state. Practitioners are not allowed to work in the National Health Service, nor are they able to sign death certificates or other similar documents. Physicians and surgeons practising orthodox medicine have often been sceptical about the claims of alternative techniques.

There are now signs that attitudes are changing. Some of the therapies like osteopathy, acupuncture and homeopathy are now acknowledged to be valuable in certain treatments. In 1983, the British Medical Association set up an investigation to enquire into fringe medicine in all its forms. One proposal is that it could be administered by qualified practitioners working alongside doctors of orthodox medicine.

61 The bones of the spinal column can clearly be ➤ seen in this X-ray photograph. X-rays were discovered by a German, Konrad Roentgen, in 1895.

Modern Medicine

In this book, most of the discoveries described were made by British medical doctors and scientists. In other countries, there have been different discoveries which help to conquer disease. Just as British advances benefit overseas doctors, so, too, discoveries like X-rays by Konrad Roentgen (1845-1923) in Germany, and radium by Pierre Curie (1858-1906) and his wife Marie Curie (1867-1934) in France, are widely used in Britain. Medicine is a universal skill, to be shared and furthered all over the world.

The story of disease and discovery is not at an end. Men and women dedicated to the art of healing still take the Hippocratic oath:

I swear and I vow . . .
I will follow that method of treatment which, according to my ability and judgment, I consider for the benefit of my patients, and abstain from whatever is deleterious and mischievous . . . .
With purity and with holiness I will pass my life and practise my art . . . .

But the art of medicine is now very much involved with science and technology.

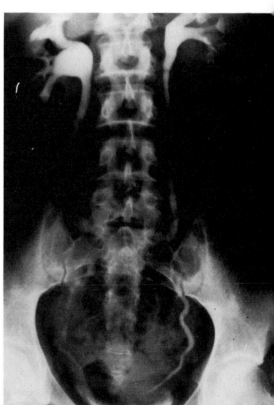

Glossary

amputation a surgical operation to cut off a diseased limb.

anaesthetic a drug used to produce unconsciousness in the whole body, or insensitivity in a specific part.

anatomy the construction of the body; also the study of the subject.

antibiotic a substance which helps to overcome germs causing infectious disease.

antiseptic a substance which kills, or prevents from multiplying, many bacteria in the air.

bacteria organisms which often cause disease but can only be seen with a microscope.

capillaries very small hair-like tubes which connect veins and arteries.

contagious applied to a disease which is spread from an infected person to a healthy one by personal contact.

diagnosis the recognition of a disease by the symptoms which are present.

dissect to cut a specimen into parts in order to examine it.

epidemic a widespread outbreak of disease.

germ a small live cell which can sometimes cause illness and which reproduces rapidly by division. It can be killed by antibiotics.

herbal a book describing the healing properties of herbs and plants.

hygiene standards of cleanliness and sanitation which contribute to the maintenance of good health.

immunise to protect from disease.

infection a disease caused by germs.

inhale to breathe in.

inoculation to inject a substance into the blood in order to protect against a disease.

insecticide something which kills insects.

malnutrition poor health brought about by insufficient or incorrect food.

microscope an instrument containing one or more lenses which magnify very tiny objects.

midwifery assistance at childbirth.

oration a formal speech or lecture.

patent medicine a medicine, often made to a secret recipe, which is protected by a patent in order to prevent others copying it.

pathology the study of the cause, effect and treatment of a disease.

pharmacy the preparation of medicines and drugs according to a doctor's prescription.

physician one who treats the sick with medicine in order to cure. A physician now also uses scientific machines and apparatus.

prognosis the indication of what is likely to happen during the course of a disease.

sallow the pale yellow colour of the complexion in certain illnesses.

septic the state of a wound when it becomes poisoned by infection.

surgeon a doctor who performs operations on the body to treat disease or injury.

therapy treatment used to overcome disease and aid recovery.

tuberculosis an infective disease caused by bacteria, which seriously affects, and sometimes consumes, the lungs or other parts of the body.

virus a chemical substance which is not alive but which, like a germ, can cause illness and can rapidly reproduce itself. Antibiotics are ineffective against a virus.

vitamins parts of natural foods which, in minute quantities, are vital for the maintenance of good health.

zoologist one who studies animal life within the science of biology.

69

Some Key Dates

400 BC	Hippocrates works in Cos, Greece
AD 1348-50	The Black Death
1505	Edinburgh School of Surgery formed
1518	Royal College of Physicians of London granted a charter
1628	William Harvey publishes his findings on the circulation of the blood
1662	Royal Society of London for Improving Natural Knowledge granted a charter
1665	The Great Plague
1770	William Hunter's School of Anatomy founded
1796	Edward Jenner carries out the first vaccination against smallpox
1800	Humphry Davy experiments with nitrous oxide
1800	Royal College of Surgeons of England founded
1813	Elizabeth Fry first visits Newgate Jail
1846	An anaesthetic first used in an operation
1847	James Simpson publishes his findings on chloroform as an anaesthetic
1854	Florence Nightingale arrives at Scutari Hospital
1867	Joseph Lister publishes his work on antiseptic treatment
1870	Elizabeth Garrett Anderson qualifies as a doctor of medicine
1897	Ronald Ross discovers the source of malarial infection
1912	Frederick Gowland Hopkins discovers that vitamins are essential for good health
1918-19	Epidemic of Spanish Influenza
1928	Alexander Fleming discovers penicillin
1940s	Epidemic of poliomyelitis
1941	Penicillin used on humans after Howard Florey and Ernst Chain overcome the problems
1961	Thalidomide tragedy
1962	Campaign against smoking
1962	First human heart transplant

Books for Further Reading

Beverley Birch,
Marie Curie – Radium Scientist,
Macdonald Education, 1977

Alan Delgado,
As They Saw Her – Florence Nightingale,
(The Nurses with Florence Nightingale tell their story)
Geo. G. Harrap, 1970

Nance Lui Fyson,
Disease and World Health,
Batsford, 1973

Kenneth Hughes,
Ask the Lab (medical laboratory technology),
My Life and My Work series.
Educational Explorers, 1971

Manpower Services Commission,
Medicine and Surgery,
Choice of Careers booklet No.108
H.M.S.O. 1981

Lionel Rose,
Health and Hygiene,
Batsford, 1975

Eric Ryckmans,
Working with Disabled People
Batsford, 1983

Nina Sully,
Health,
Batsford, 1983

Nina Sully,
Looking at Medicine,
Batsford, 1984

B.J.Williams,
Spare Parts for People,
Wayland, 1978

Index

The numerals in **bold** type refer to the figure numbers of the illustrations